# STARTING
## *Again*

lip

First published in 2015 by:

Live It Publishing
27 Old Gloucester Road
London, United Kingdom.
WC1N 3AX

www.liveitpublishing.com
Copyright © 2015 by Jackie Mendoza

Although every effort has been made to ensure the accuracy of the
information, advice and instructions contained in this book, it is sold
with the understanding that neither the author nor the publisher are
giving specific diagnostic or treatment advice. Each person has unique
needs and  circumstances that can present complex issues that are
beyond the scope of this book. For specific advice, the reader is
advised to consult a coach or therapist.

All enquiries should be addressed to Live It Publishing.

ISBN: 978-1-910565-11-7 (pbk)
All available as eBook

# CONTENTS

Introduction: My story                                          1

Chapter 1: What do you want?                                   15

Chapter 2: What's stopping you?                                39

Chapter 3: Beliefs                                             47

Chapter 4: The limiting beliefs that are stopping you         55

Chapter 5: Positive intent                                    63

Chapter 6: Creating or updating beliefs                       75

Chapter 7: Learning to be at peace with yourself              85

Chapter 8: Conclusion                                        107

# ACKNOWLEDGEMENTS

THIS book and my journey so far would not have been possible without the support, wonderful humour and wisdom of a whole host of inspirational teachers. Amongst them I'd particularly like to mention Annie Bowen, Barbara Somers, Ian McDermott, Prof Patricia Riddell, Suzi Smith, Tim Hallbom and Robert Dilts.

I'd like to extend a special thank you to Ian, Tim and Robert as a few of the techniques they shared at International Teaching Seminars' NLP Master Practitioner Certification Programme are mentioned in this book and are indeed used regularly by me in my coaching work.

Thank you too to fellow coach Teak Rehman whose insights and playful sense of humour have skilfully supported me through this new part of my journey, to my copy editor Brian Burns who taught me a fair deal about getting a manuscript ready for publishing and to my publisher Murielle Maupoint for making my first foray into the world of publishing so enjoyable and easy.

Last but not least, I dedicate this book to my beautiful wife Sue for all her continued love, support, honesty and encouragement and to all of my readers for their courage to start again.

# MY STORY

UNTIL I reached the age of 47, I felt as if I'd spent most of my adult life not really knowing what I wanted and forever trying to live up to other people's expectations.

On the face of it, I had an amazing and seemingly privileged childhood. I grew up in different countries and cultures, and my parents made sure I went to the best schools. Because I was an only child, everyone tended to assume that I was spoilt and given all the attention I ever wanted.

I did get attention but most of the time it wasn't the type that I craved. My parents had grown up with their own inherited sets of beliefs, values and conditioning. These combined to create a particular world view that focused on lack (your typical glass half empty vs half full) and life's worst-case scenarios, and was characterised by an acute concern for what other people might think.

Growing up in this reality meant I was lucky enough to have most of what I needed in terms of material things. My parents showed their love for me in this way, but not in terms of emotional presence, support and encouragement. My memories of early childhood are less about quality and fun time spent with my parents, and more about being told off or being smacked for doing something wrong. So, from a very early age, as I absorbed more and more of their punishing words and smacks, I gradually formed a sense of not ever being good enough and having to constantly put other people's expectations before my own.

When I started school, that feeling of not being good enough translated into a strong need to prove myself. Some would say this is a good thing – after all, what's wrong with being a conscientious and driven pupil at school? Conscientious and driven children surely become driven and successful adults, right?

But all I can remember of my school days was

the constant pressure to do well. It was as if I simply couldn't ever go home with bad grades. When it came to mathematics, my worst subject, I was driven to cheating in tests rather than face the humiliation of my parents' disappointment or anger. It never occurred to me that they'd be even more disappointed and angry if they found out I'd cheated. Out of desperation to avoid the immediate repercussions of bad grades, I felt I had no choice but to resort to cheating. And it didn't matter to me that the maths genius I was copying from sussed what I was doing – I just had to continue doing it and hope he didn't have the guts to tell on me. This was pure self-preservation – do or 'die' at the thought of my parents' disappointment and yet another reason not to feel good enough.

Eventually, my childhood logic equated praise for doing well at school with being loved, regardless of how I achieved that praise. After all, this was the only time I ever got positive attention from my parents. In the end, I transferred this logic and behaviour onto my teachers and other grown-ups: I am only good if I do well in other people's eyes and live my life according to their tune.

## Enter the perfectionist

Because I'd never grown up with a sense of being good enough just for being me, I ended up constantly needing that validation from other people. I was never able to give it to myself… and so the perfectionist was born.

Earlier this year when I read one of Brené Brown's definitions of perfectionism in her wonderful book Daring Greatly[1], a huge part of my life and 'dysfunction' suddenly acquired new and deeper meaning. It was an immense 'a-ha' moment:

*Perfectionism is, at its core, about trying to earn approval. Most perfectionists grew up being praised for achievement and performance (grades, manners, rule following, people pleasing, appearance, sports). Somewhere along the way they adopted this dangerous and debilitating belief system: "I am what I accomplish and how well I accomplish it.…Healthy striving is self-focused: how can I improve? Perfectionism is others-focused: What will they think? Perfectionism is a hustle.[2]*

'Perfectionism is others-focused' – all of a sudden, a major part of my life and the reason why I had been so fundamentally unhappy revealed itself in glorious technicolour. It was a dangerous and debilitating belief system along with the others I'd inherited from my parents: the glass is always half empty, never half full, and worst-case scenarios which for me translated into 'the world is an unsafe place'.

Weighed down by those beliefs, it's no wonder I stumbled through life the way I did. I now understand how the pressure of never being good enough in others' eyes fuelled my sometimes deep and near destructive depression in adolescence. A good few years of counselling, psychotherapy and spiritual healing thankfully saw me through to becoming what I'd term 'a generally functioning yet dysfunctional adult'.

I say 'generally functioning' because outwardly I was doing really well. I was still getting the good 'grades' in the form of good jobs, my own flat, a nice car – but my often difficult, sometimes destructive, relationships with others and my inability to find the special, loving relationship that I craved so much showed how dysfunctional my inner world still was.

## Silly little things

Looking back, I'd say spiritual healing helped me begin to explore the whole alien concept of being present for, and looking after, myself. To this day I remember how sceptical I felt when Annie, my healer, encouraged me to do 'silly little things' like buy myself flowers, have a candle-lit bath, cook myself a lovely meal, set aside regular time for meditation or just sit and look at the moon and stars. 'Yeah, right, how the hell's that going to help?' I thought to myself while smiling and nodding at her suggestions.

Luckily, and perhaps because I felt desperate, having run out of all other possibilities, I decided to give the 'hocus-pocus, airy-fairy nonsense' a try. That, and my first foray into transpersonal psychology (often known as 'spiritual' psychology), were bids to find a way out of the depression and hopelessness that I'd taken into adulthood, despite the outer trappings of 'success'.

Something definitely worked, because after years spent chasing the wrong people and/or embarking on very short and often destructive relationships, at the age of 34, I finally met my partner and now wife, Sue.

Although our relationship had its stormy ups and downs at the beginning (we were both perfectionists in our own unique ways, after all), finally having the loving relationship I'd craved gave me the sense of safety and ultimate balance that I felt I'd never had before.

## Striking out on my own

While my private life was settling down, parts of my inner dysfunction (the crippling beliefs in lack, perfectionism and worst-case scenarios) were still playing out in my work. I jumped from job to job never quite lasting beyond two years. My excuses ranged from being ambitious and therefore needing to move somewhere else to get the promotion, through not wanting to work for bosses who were out to make my life a complete misery, to working for organisations that were dysfunctional and unwilling to change. In each case it was someone else's fault, but never mine – of course.

Then, in 2007, I finally had the guts to go freelance. I started my own consultancy/interim management business, which of course, being the perfectionist and high achiever that I was, was very successful. I certainly made a good living out of it and because I was effectively self-employed, it meant I finally had the perfect excuse to carry on job-hopping whenever I wanted or needed to. I'd finally created the perfect work scenario for myself. Or so I thought.

As if by magic, though, the same scenarios that had been playing out in my permanent roles suddenly started appearing in my interim roles. Shit! Nowhere to run now. It all came to a head when I turned 45.

## The turning point

I'll always remember the run-up to my 45th birthday, because at times it felt as if the depression and hopelessness I'd carried around with me in adolescence and early adulthood was rearing its ugly head again. It started with a dull dissatisfaction in the background, followed by a general 'scratchiness' with the outside world. Luckily, my earlier years of therapy and healing, together with the training I'd done, meant I wasn't going to let myself ignore the warning signs altogether. Besides, deep down I was shit scared of getting deeply depressed again.

When the 'scratchiness' began to feel like downright irritability with almost everything around me, I decided to contact my healer Annie again. I hadn't seen her for almost 13 years, not since Sue and I had got together and my life had finally begun to feel safer and more balanced. Seeing Annie and receiving healing once again, it felt as if I'd come full circle, which I guess I had, in a funny sort of way. My session helped me come to terms with the fact I was going through my own mid-life crisis. And this particular crisis was urgently pressing me to bring more meaning and depth into my life. In effect, it was pushing me to start again.

Exploring what 'meaning' and 'depth' meant to me, and how I might have lost them along the way, made me realise that while I was still busy striving for perfection in my chosen career, I'd slowly let go of my passion for psychology and what makes people tick. That was a massive realisation in itself because it showed me where I needed to search and it ultimately led me to Neuro-Linguistic Programming (NLP) with Ian McDermott. Often described as 'the study of the structure of subjective experience', NLP helps people develop the right tools and resources to think, behave and communicate effectively, so that they can achieve specific goals.

I'd wanted to take part in an NLP Practitioner programme for a while but had never got round to it. This time, I asked for recommendations and booked myself onto the next available course. It was one of the best things I've ever done for myself.

First and most importantly, the programme drove home to me the sheer power of our minds and thoughts, and the meaning we decide to give those thoughts. I began to realise that when we're able to manage our minds and thoughts better, we begin to have more choices. It's the difference between choosing to react in anger or choosing to respond calmly; choosing to take a comment personally or choosing to believe the comment wasn't intended to cause offence in the first place.

I also learnt that the past doesn't have to rule the present and that I can choose whether to make this true for myself or not. The scary thing is, I soon realised just how much my past was still ruling my present. When the full impact of that realisation began to sink in, there was no way I could allow it to continue.

Looking at my beliefs and how they influenced the way I went about the world brought me to the shocking realisation that most of the beliefs I was carrying around didn't even belong to me. They were my mum's or my dad's, yet I'd taken them on as my own and in doing so I was affecting the very quality and potential of *my* life experience. The greatest feeling of freedom came from knowing I no longer needed to carry those beliefs with me because I could update those beliefs or create new ones that better suited who I was.

The programme was transformational because I finally felt I had a better handle on who I truly was and, more importantly, who I could yet become. There was no way I could go through an experience like that without it filtering through into every other area of my life.

Those five months of input, fully immersive exercises where we practised various trans-formational techniques, and the encouragement (and permission) to 'dare to dream', inevitably made it more and more difficult for me to go back into the same old, same old of my daily work routine. Long before I'd started NLP, I'd already felt unease and discomfort. But while I was taking part in the programme, enjoying an environment in which I was present and more true to myself, it became increasingly difficult to switch back to the normal routine of simply going through the motions. Gradually, the unease and discomfort became more acute. This conflict in my life was really beginning to get under my skin.

## Starting again

Elsewhere, though, wonderful things were happening. Sue and I got married and we headed off to Florida for our honeymoon. Taking nearly three weeks out of our day-to-day routine was exactly what I needed to find the space and distance to take stock. I'd loaded up my Kindle with a series of self-help and personal development books that really got me thinking about what I truly wanted from my life. I'd spent most of my working life helping causes succeed, but I still didn't know what my own cause in life was.

The answer was quite simple: from then on I wanted to live life to my full potential because I realised I'd been compromising myself and my dreams in order to 'fit in'. Fitting in had given me great job titles, good money, a lovely house, a cool car and endless stuff to prove I'd reached a certain level in life. But was I *really* happy? Did I really feel present, alive and engaged in my own life? The sad answer was: no.

Was I prepared to continue living like this for the rest of my life? Categorically no. Something had to give. And it did.

On the morning of my first day back to work, as I ate my cereal, staring out into the dark autumn morning, getting ready to brave the cold, then squeeze into a stuffy train packed with commuters, I suddenly thought: what the hell am I doing? Is this what I signed up for? Is this why I chose to go freelance? Just to carry on with a monotonous routine of working four days a week (yippee!) instead of five?

I immediately made a pact with myself. I committed to breaking out of the routine of 'fitting in' and to allowing myself to start over and live my life on my own terms. As much as I wanted to live my life to my full potential, I also knew my personal cause was to help others do the same.

When I started my coaching practice, I began to see a pattern in the clients I was seeing. Most of them were women at quarter-life or mid-life stages. Some were coming out of long-term relationships, some were having to come to terms with their children growing up and no longer needing them so much, while others were realising their chosen career paths were no longer fulfilling them. In all cases, each woman was needing to find herself and start again.

This book, therefore, sets out the steps I personally took to achieve that. I have subsequently taken many clients successfully through those same steps to help them finally find their purpose or create a new one to fit the next stage of their lives.

In the following pages, you'll learn how to state your purpose, know what's important to you, embrace your gifts and talents, create new beliefs about yourself and take purposeful action. You'll also learn the true meaning of living at peace with yourself so that you can, at last, begin to feel much more present, connected and engaged with everyone and everything around you.

1. Brene Brown. *Daring Greatly – How the Courage to Be Vulnerable Transforms the Way We Live, Love, Parent and Lead.* Penguin
2. *The Shield: Perfectionism,* Chapter 4

CHAPTER **1**

# WHAT DO YOU WANT?

*Better to have a short life that is full of what you like doing than a long life spent in a miserable way.*

Alan Watts

IN order to fill your life with what you like doing, you need to know what it is you really want. So tell me, how often have you stopped to ask yourself this question: what do I want?

Personally, I only learnt to ask myself that question on a consistent basis when I turned 45 and was already studying Neuro-Linguistic Programming (NLP). Before that, like many other people, I simply launched into things on automatic pilot. I may have been asked a weak variation of that question when I was at school, ie, what do you want to do when you grow up? But the question was loaded with academic expectation. I knew that my answer was meant to spell out what I was going to study at university. And back then, what did I know? At one point I wanted to become a biochemist, then an actress and then a simultaneous interpreter. Of those three, in terms of creativity, character analysis and being able to put myself in someone else's shoes, actress may be the closest to what I do now…but only just.

Those were career decisions, but what about those seemingly simple decisions we make every day? Do you really believe what you say or do you say it because you're worried what other people think? For example, do you really want to go to the party or do you end up going because that's what your friends always expect you to do? Do you really want to take on another project or do you agree because you don't want to let everyone else down?

Because we seldom ask ourselves what we want and what we truly desire, it's no wonder the video of the question 'What do you desire?'

by philosopher Alan Watts did the rounds on YouTube and touched many people on social media channels in late 2012. If you haven't seen it already, be sure to seek it out.

Perhaps that video captured so many hearts and minds because it awoke us to the realisation that we're not used to asking ourselves what we really want and, even if we do, we seldom dare truly listen to ourselves and answer authentically from our core.

So why is it important to ask ourselves what we want on a regular and consistent basis?

Because by doing so:

- We connect more with what we really want rather than what we think other people expect from us
- We connect more with who we truly are
- We begin to feel more focused and to find direction – it's the difference between living with purpose and living on automatic pilot.

Now let's try it on for size. Clear some time and space to explore and be curious. Ask yourself: if money and time were no object, what would I want?

The question can be as broad or as specific as you want. You may choose to focus on what you want from a particular situation or you may want to explore what you want in life right now. Whichever you choose, note down what it is you really want.

Once you've made a note of what you want, allow yourself to play and explore even further. Now imagine you have what you want – allow your imagination to take you wherever it wants to. What do you see, hear and feel as you experience and connect with what you *really* want? Immerse yourself as fully as you can in that experience. See what you see, hear what you hear and feel what you feel. By immersing yourself, you're beginning to make what you want more vivid and tangible. You are breathing more life and feeling into your goal.

Once you've fully connected with the experience of what you really want, take notes or write down your experience in detail. As you've connected fully with the experience, know you can return to it whenever you wish. If you like to meditate, spend some quiet time alone or simply daydream, these are good times to relive your experience.

## Why do you want it?

If we seldom ask ourselves what we want, then we very rarely ask ourselves *why* we want it.

'Why?' is another very important question. Asking why we want something gives our goals meaning and purpose, and, as human beings, we're constantly yearning for both. In fact, the more compelling the meaning or purpose for us, the stronger we'll fight for it.

Most New Year's resolutions fail because we haven't made them compelling enough. All too often we make resolutions such as 'I'm going to lose weight', 'I'm going to give up smoking', 'I'm going to exercise more' or 'I'm going to cut down on my drinking'. But how many times have we actually followed through? If we're lucky, maybe, we stick it out to the end of February, but rarely beyond. If a goal or resolution isn't important or compelling enough for us, we've got little reason to follow through, apart perhaps from a little peer pressure here and there.

## The power of the compelling goal

I learnt the power of a compelling goal the hard way about seven Christmases ago. I've often struggled with my weight and while I've always been into exercise and keeping fit, there came a time seven years ago when the weight simply piled on and wouldn't shift, no matter how often I went to the gym. If I'm honest I think I'd managed to fool myself into thinking that because I exercised more regularly than most people I knew, I could afford to eat as much as I wanted because I was burning it off. Wrong. A photograph my wife took of me that Christmas was all the evidence I needed. I. Was. Big.

At first I went into denial. How could this be? It must be the angle the photograph was taken at. I'm not actually that big in real life! But then I slowly realised I'd probably been avoiding really looking at myself in the mirror, and that I'd been favouring looser clothes to those that were beginning to feel very tight. I was a master of denial back then. But no amount of denial could hide the compelling visual evidence of my weight gain staring at me out of that photograph.

After the self-loathing I felt for 'letting myself go' the way I did, I finally took another long look at the photograph and at myself in the mirror. It helped that I'd just turned 40 that month. Having reached that important milestone, my choices became clear: either commit to doing something about your weight now and choose good health as you grow older; or carry on as you are and seriously risk your health. There's a history of obesity-related illness on my dad's side of the family, so that gave me some added incentive.

As the New Year began, I trawled through the classifieds of our local magazine and found myself a personal trainer. I lost more than a stone in weight and went from struggling to catch my breath after running a couple of metres up the road, to completing half marathons. That's the power of a compelling goal.

## Finding reasons that grab

With that in mind, take another look at what you want and now note down the reasons why you want it. Your reasons need to be compelling and powerful. They need to grab at you so much that you simply cannot wait to take action to make it happen.

If you're struggling to find compelling reasons, you may want to reconsider what you said you want – is it *truly* what you want? Did you say you wanted it because that's what your partner/

parents/siblings/children/friends/colleagues would expect you to say? What does the real you want?

If you absolutely know it's what you want but you still find it difficult to think of a compelling reason to make it happen, try this:

Close your eyes and imagine what it will be like if you don't make the change you say you want by next year? How do you see yourself? What are you feeling? How does your body feel? What are you hearing? What if you don't make that change you say you want in three years, in five years, in 10 years, in 20 years? What will life be like if you carry on as you are and don't make that change in 20 years?

When I do this exercise with people, more often than not, at the 20-year mark, they say: 'I may as well be dead.' Is that a compelling enough reason for you?

## What if you don't know what you want?

I've worked with a number of people who've drawn a blank when I've asked them what they want. More often than not they'll shrug their shoulders, sigh deeply and say: 'That's the problem. I just don't know what I want.' It's as if all passion and energy has slowly leaked out of their very core because they've spent so much of their lives putting other people's needs and expectations above their own.

If this is true for you, a journey of rediscovery is needed. In fact, rediscovering yourself is a useful and powerful exercise for everyone, regardless of whether or not you're already in tune with what you really want. Who knows what new discoveries you might make.

### Discovering your values

Values are significant because they're our own personal and individual beliefs about what's most important to us. In fact, they're specific, highly emotional and connected beliefs that determine how we respond to any given situation in life. From how we dress to what we eat, where we live, who we hang out with, who we fall in love with, what we do for a living and where we choose to work – our values rule every area of our lives. Ironically, they can be so ingrained that we're almost unaware of them until we're openly encouraged to explore them.

It was only when I actively explored my values that I eventually realised why I never seemed to stay in a job longer than two years. One of my key values is integrity and by that I mean: being true to myself and to others. When I commit to doing something, I will do my very best to do it and provide evidence of my actions. In many work situations though, I found this value was rarely shared by others. Time and time again, I'd feel disappointed because bosses or colleagues would say one thing quite convincingly and then do the exact opposite or take no action at all. I'd end up getting extremely frustrated, burn out and eventually leave. I'd come up with all sorts of reasons why it didn't work out, mainly blaming 'them' for being weak, unreasonable, lacking integrity – you name it. What I didn't know, until much later, was that there was a mismatch of values: mine didn't match theirs.

As well as identifying what my values were, I did some healing work around why certain values (for me, integrity) could be so highly charged. And once I did that, I began to experience the world around me with a much lighter touch. Recognising that certain situations or relationships don't work or flow because of a mismatch of values helps me to take things less personally. It also helps me attract and focus on the relationships and situations that are right for, or in line with, who I am.

With this in mind, ask yourself now: what are my values? To start exploring these, let's hone in on key areas of you life. Your values don't have to be a single word – they can be a phrase or sentence. Note down whatever works for you and bear in mind that you may well have similar values in each area:

### Relationships

*What's most important to you when you're relating to others?*

**Family**

*What's most important to you about family?*

## Work

*What's most important to you about the work you do?*

## Environment

*What's most important to you about the environment you live and work in?*

## Wellbeing and happiness

*What's most important to you in terms of your general wellbeing and happiness?*

Keep your list of values somewhere safe. You'll find you have some core values and others that shift as you yourself change. Your list of values is a work in progress and it's useful to revisit it regularly because, as Tony Robbins, says: '... it's important to learn what your values are so you will be able to direct, motivate and support yourself at the deepest level.'[1]

Knowing what your values are is an important step to truly getting to know yourself. As you do that, you begin to get a feel for what it is you want.

### What are you good at?

It's well known that as human beings we're better at identifying what we're not good at than we are at finding what we are good at. Go figure. We're so used to looking for the bad points that we often ignore, or are completely blind to, the good bits. No wonder we end up losing ourselves to the point that we no longer know what we want. After all, losers don't deserve what they want, right?

Let's turn that on its head right now. In this section I'm inviting you to do something new. I want you to concentrate on what you are good at. Yes, you read that right – what you're *good* at. To do that, I want you to remember the compliments that other people have paid you. Why? Because those compliments are a very good indication of where our strengths lie, yet most of us lose sight of that because we're too busy brushing them aside or just plain ignoring them. And guess what? Focusing on what you're good at often gives you clues to what you could and should be doing more of in life – and those clues can eventually lead you to what you want.

So, what have people said you're good at? Go as far back as you like and make sure you also note down the reasons why people said you are good at something. See how many examples you can add in the following table:

| What? | Why? |
|---|---|
| For example: advising people what to do | Because I have helped them figure out problems |
| | |
| | |
| | |
| | |
| | |
| | |
| | |
| | |
| | |
| | |
| | |
| | |
| | |
| | |
| | |
| | |
| | |
| | |
| | |
| | |
| | |
| | |
| | |
| | |
| | |
| | |
| | |
| | |
| | |

### *What were you passionate about as a child?*

Children have a wonderful capacity for spontaneity, imagination, creativity and play. It's just a shame that most of us dilute those gifts when we grow up, as we learn to conform to what's expected of us as adults.

When I was a kid, I invented an amazing imaginary life for myself, partly because I was an only child and partly because I wanted to escape from a not so happy childhood. I loved books and writing from a very early age and I remember making my own books and magazines – sheets of paper with lots of stories and, sometimes, pictures that I'd bind myself. I even remember 'inventing' a car that could carry a yacht in its undercarriage and trying to convince my friends at school of its existence by showing them 'brochures' (pictures I'd drawn myself), but I remember how utterly convinced I was that everyone else would believe it was real.

In fact, as a child, I certainly had a great passion for creativity, story-telling and imagining other people's lives. As an adult I know I thrive best when I have room to create and to take in others' creativity. I'm lucky in that most of the jobs I've done have involved a certain level of creativity. Indeed, story-telling and my childhood passion for imagining other people's lives (and, in effect, placing myself in another's person's shoes) translated into my passion for psychology and later NLP.

I like to call our childhood passions our hidden treasures because they can be just that – a light shining on core passions we need to reconnect with and make more prominent in our adult lives.

Now think back to your childhood. What did you enjoy doing as a child?

Once you've done that, take some time to remember: what did you dream of becoming when you grew up?

## Bringing the strands together

Exploring your values, identifying what other people say you're good at, uncovering your hidden treasures – all of these can provide clues about your (often hidden) self. Now, here's what you can do with the information you've gathered above.

## Make sure your values are reflected in the key areas of your life

For me, that often meant walking away from situations or people I felt were no longer in synch with my values. It also meant learning to say 'no'. Sure, it was scary at first, but, in time, as I learnt to honour my values and subsequently myself more, I began to attract the people and situations more in synch with where I was at and what I wanted to be in life. The pay-off was that I became a much happier person as every area of my life felt more in balance.

## Start to think how you can incorporate your hidden treasures into your life

Trudi (not her real name), a client of mine, came to me because she felt stuck in a rut and had lost a sense of direction in her life. She was holding down two part-time jobs, one she wasn't enjoying anymore and one that she generally liked but wasn't quite sure about as a long-term career.

In our sessions, during the hidden treasures exercise, it became clear that Trudi had a deep passion and gifts for playing the viola da gamba and for illustrating. Yet these two things hardly figured in her life. In fact, they'd been pushed way into the background. I worked with Trudi to reconnect her with her passions in a real way and to explore how she could incorporate them more into her daily life. Within a month she'd made time to revisit and tidy her studio, and get started on some new illustrations. Soon after, she resigned from the job she didn't like, got one that suited her better and gave her time to devote to her art. In a matter of months Trudi's life became purposeful again.

How can you do the same by embracing your hidden treasures?

### *Do more of the things you're good at*

Are the things you're good at a key part of how you make a living? If not, start exploring how they can be. Start with little things and gradually build things up. For example, if people have commented that you're really good at listening and giving sound advice, are you doing that in some shape or form at work? If not, could you? Is there a specific project you could lead on or get involved with? Is there a mentoring programme you could sign up for? And if not, could you volunteer for a mentoring programme outside of work?

By acknowledging, embracing and doing more of what you're good at, not only are you getting to do more of what you enjoy, but you're also opening yourself up to opportunities for more of the same.

My life certainly felt more meaningful and charged when I was truly able to take what I'm good at and use it in my work to make a real difference by helping people transform their lives.

1 Robbins, A. 1986 *Unlimited Power – The New Science of Personal Achievement* (iPad edition), page 412

# Chapter 2

# WHAT'S STOPPING YOU?

NOW that you know what you want, what's stopping you from getting it?

Just as we're all really good at focusing on our bad points and ignoring the good bits, when it comes to why we can't have what we want, most of us are equally talented at coming up with a hundred and one different reasons, excuses or 'stories'. That's precisely why a lot of us say we want to change, state what it is we want to change, maybe even list how we're going to change, but never quite seem to get past the first few hurdles: because the reasons, excuses and stories we tell ourselves take over and take charge.

Let's put it to the test right now. Take a look again at what you said you want. Now be really honest with yourself. When you look at what you want, what are the reasons, excuses or stories that you come up with to explain why you can't have what you want? List them now:

Why is it that all these reasons and stories pop into our minds so easily? Because we've become experts at limiting ourselves through our negative beliefs and the critical self-talk that goes with them. Quite simply, most of us have lost the capacity we had as children to imagine, create, and believe anything is possible, so we automatically default to the opposite position and even create excuses to support this lack of belief. Let's face it, until some adult or older kid tells them otherwise, most younger kids still believe a large man from Lapland in a red suit, with white hair and a beard, delivers their presents every Christmas. Or that the tooth fairy leaves money under the pillow when they lose a tooth. We all believed in magic of some kind until we had to grow up. As Marianne Williamson, the spiritual teacher and author, once said: 'Children are happy because they don't have a file in their minds called All the Things That Could Go Wrong.'

## The loss of magic

To this day I remember the moment I found out Santa Claus didn't exist. I don't know how old I was but I remember exactly how I felt. Until that point I'd religiously write out my letter to Santa every year, telling him how I'd been good and what I wanted for Christmas. Every year, I'd excitedly give my letter to my dad to post and then the eager anticipation would begin, building up to sheer excitement on the evening of the 24th and exhilaration on the day itself. I totally believed that Santa existed and that Rudolph and the reindeers pulled his sleigh.

Then, one day, as I was playing with a friend, I got to talking about what I'd asked Santa for Christmas. My not-so-much-older but decidedly wiser friend rolled his eyes before dropping the bomb: 'You do know Santa Claus doesn't exist, right?'

'Of course he does!'

'No he doesn't. Santa Claus is your mum and dad. They're the ones that give you presents. Can't believe you didn't know *that*!'

From that moment on, it was as if my whole world had suddenly fallen apart. I didn't want to believe my friend, but I began to piece together little snippets I'd chosen to ignore before – the time I'd found my letter to Santa open in my dad's jacket pocket or the glimpse I had of my dad taking some presents out of his and mum's bedroom on Christmas Eve night. When eventually I had the guts to confront my mum and dad with my discovery, and when they admitted the truth of it, I was completely and utterly gutted. I felt cheated too. From then on, I gradually stopped believing in magic.

## How we limit ourselves

In workshops I illustrate how growing up, and our mastery of self-limitation, follows a similar pattern.

We all come into this world as innocent, trusting, loving and open little beings with a will to believe that anything and everything is possible. Our very core is made up of innocence, trust, love and openness. But as we go through life and grow up, that core is influenced by the beliefs, values, thoughts and behaviours of the adults around us – our parents, guardians, grandparents, aunts, uncles and teachers all contribute to how we see, feel and hear the world around us. Gradually, often without even being consciously aware of it, we 'take on' their beliefs, thoughts and behaviours, and they stack up over our core. We begin to compile that file in our minds (and it's a hefty one) called 'All the

Things That Could go Wrong'.

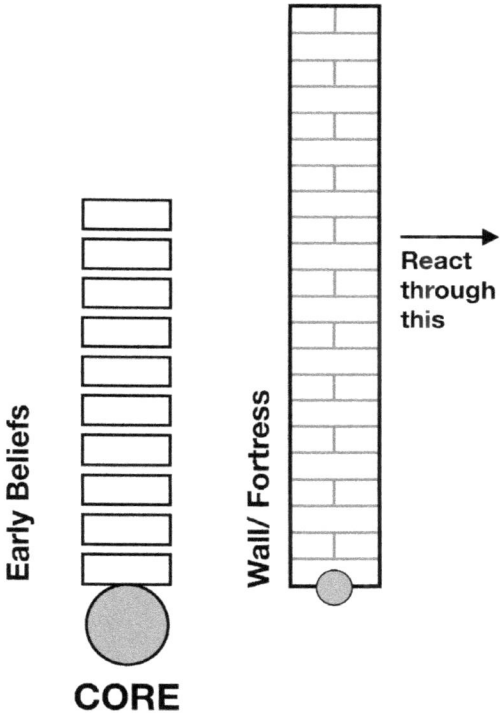

As the years go by, the stacked-up beliefs grow stronger and more solid. Before we know it, that little makeshift barrier of 'belief bricks' becomes a sturdy wall or fortress we react or respond through. Our core is still there but it's been squashed to a dot.

Unless we question the beliefs we're carrying around, they start to limit us and weigh us down. They're responsible for the host of reasons, excuses and stories we use to explain why we can't have or achieve what we want. Life begins to feel flat, as if we're not living, but merely existing.

# CHAPTER 3

# BELIEFS

*It's not the events of our lives that shape us, but our beliefs as to what those events mean.*

Tony Robbins

BELIEFS are a funny thing. On the one hand, they can bring purpose to our lives; on the other, they can seriously limit the extent to which we experience life. That's why I love the above quote from Tony Robbins. Events don't shape us – it's our beliefs about the meaning of those events that do. Despite the sheer power beliefs can have over our lives, it's a shame that very few of us actually take the time to explore and question them.

When I eventually dug deep to discover and look at my own beliefs, the whole process blew my mind. That's not surprising – after all, I'd never questioned my beliefs. Why the hell would I? They were how I lived my life. They gave me the framework for how I experienced my life and were everything I held to be true. Why would I want to question that? I'm glad I did, however, because I soon discovered that as much as some of my beliefs were guiding me through life relatively well, others were seriously limiting me and, in some cases, making my life and the lives of everyone around me a misery.

If you find yourself feeling stuck, stagnant and fed up because you keep doing those same old things you keep telling yourself you want to stop doing, then it's time to look at your beliefs.

## Beliefs are not reality

The one thing to bear in mind is that beliefs are *about* reality, not reality itself. That thought alone fascinated me because I soon realised, if that's the case, then surely we can all change how we experience our reality by changing our beliefs about it?

Let's try a little experiment. Two people hold contrasting beliefs:

- The world is an unsafe place *vs* The world is a safe place

- People always let you down *vs* There's good in everyone

- The world's out to get me *vs* I create my own luck in the world

- Money is the root of all evil *vs* Money brings freedom

- Life's a bitch and then you die *vs* Life's a journey of discovery.

Imagine what life would be like with the first set of beliefs. Really try to see what it's like to believe that the world is unsafe and out to get you, that people always let you down, that money is the root of all evil and that, hey, life really is a bitch and then you die.

How do you feel as you carry those beliefs around? What do you hear around you? How is the world responding to you when you believe all of that? How does your body feel?

Now imagine what life's like with the second set of beliefs. Really try to see what it's like to live in a safe place where the people around you are supportive; what it's like to believe you create your own luck and wealth and that life's a journey of discoveries. What do you see, hear and feel around you? How do you feel inside and how do you go about life as you carry these beliefs with you?

Now tell me which beliefs you would choose to carry around. Unless you're addicted to pain and negativity, I'm guessing you'd choose the second set of beliefs, right? So how on earth did these two people create and develop such opposing sets of beliefs?

## When ideas become beliefs become truths

I have to admit, until I committed to discovering and questioning my own beliefs, I held most of the first set above. When I boiled it down to why I did that, it was definitely because of the *meanings* I had chosen to give, or had learned to give, to my experiences. Let's take the first belief: the world is an unsafe place.

Intuitively, I'd say I began to experience the

world as an unsafe place when I was three and my mother was diagnosed with cancer and hospitalised. I'm sure to this day that my parents believe I was unaffected by that incident but, after the many counselling and therapy sessions I've had over the years, I know differently. I know a lot of the insecurities and fears I developed were rooted in that experience. Put simply: as a three-year-old I picked up on the worry, anxiety and stress around me when my mother was hospitalised, and because I didn't know any better, I interpreted it all as evidence that something was different, not right and not safe about my world. That was the first 'imprint' experience.

Luckily, my mother survived and came home, and life gradually got back to 'normal'. But because of her own upbringing and life experience, my mother's default state was often one of fear, which translated into the generalised belief: the world is an unsafe place. This belief was then reflected in her thoughts, behaviour and responses.

What effect do you think that would have on a young child who's already created the idea of 'my world is not safe'? Would it dilute the idea or reinforce it? Over the years it would reinforce it to the point where the initial idea becomes a belief. Then, as more time passes, that belief becomes a truth. It's become such an intrinsic part of our life and experience that we no longer bother to question it. It simply becomes our reality, our view of how the world is. Because it's become so entrenched, we even go out of our way sometimes to look for evidence to back it up.

### From little seeds

How do you turn a thought or idea into a belief? Imagine a thought or idea as a little seed. You decide you're quite taken with this seed and you'd like to see it grow. So you find some nutrient-rich soil that you instinctively know carries the same 'charge' as the seed and you carefully plant it in a window box and give it all the care and attention it deserves. This seed is important to you, so you tend to it and water it until it grows strong. Because it's growing in the right environment, nurtured through all the attention you've given it, you soon see a seedling sprouting up. You feel really encouraged by this, so you carry on giving it all the attention and care it deserves. You feed it and water it. Maybe you even talk to it.

Soon, friends, family and acquaintances are drawn to what you're doing. It resonates with them, so they bring their own 'like-minded' seeds for you to plant in your window box and tend with equal care. In time, your seedling grows stronger and taller and begins to bud. Not only has it had so much care and attention from you, it's also been encouraged to grow strong by all the similar 'like-minded' plants around it. This is how – given proper nurturing and encouragement – ideas can blossom into beliefs.

Some beliefs are useful, so we want to cultivate them and keep them growing strong in their original window box. Other beliefs may be limiting or even 'out of date', so we may decide to take a cutting and plant it in a different window box with different soil and surrounding plants, to see what might happen (for more on this, see Chapter 6).

## *What are beliefs?*

Beliefs are generalisations about your experience: people always let you down, I always get a cold in winter, I never have enough time. As it's pretty impossible to know everything about any situation, we often stop looking for more information or evidence and create a belief instead. That's why it's worth redefining beliefs as: *our best current thinking.*

Beliefs are generally unconscious patterns that influence how we structure our lives. They define what we can or can't do now and what we can or can't do in the future. They tell us what to pay attention to and what to ignore. We act as if our beliefs are true.

# CHAPTER 4

# THE LIMITING BELIEFS THAT ARE STOPPING YOU

SO far we've explored what beliefs are and how we develop, nurture and 'grow' them. We also know that some beliefs are useful whereas others are limiting and/or out of date. And it's the limiting beliefs that are responsible for the reasons, excuses and stories we use to tell ourselves why we can't have what we want and why we can't start over again.

Now let's look back at the list you put together in Chapter 2 (page 40). What reasons, excuses and stories did you list for why you can't have what you want? What would you say are the limiting beliefs behind them?

When I do this exercise in workshops, some

people find it difficult to identify their limiting belief. This is perfectly normal because often the limiting beliefs that affect us the most sit outside of our conscious awareness. To see if this is happening, try some 'excavation' work. For example, when I finally realised my passion was to work as a change coach, I came up with loads of reasons and stories why it could never happen, including:

- It's difficult to start a new business

- It's difficult to start a private practice from scratch

- I won't have enough clients because people don't want to spend money on coaching

- I haven't got any money to spend on marketing

- I don't have enough time to develop the business properly

- And on and on and on...

You could say these are limiting beliefs in themselves but the trick is to get to the core belief beneath them. In other words, the one belief that acts like a thought virus and can end up infecting every single area of your life. If the core limiting belief isn't obvious at first, do some digging and start exploring the excuses you've come up with. Ask yourself why you've come up with a particular excuse, for example:

It's difficult to start a new business

*Why?*

Because I don't know what I'm doing, because I'm new to this arena, because it's not familiar, because I've got no idea where to start

It's difficult to start a private practice from scratch...

*Why?*

Because I'll have to find new clients and I don't know where to start, because I don't know how to get new clients...

I won't have enough clients because people don't want to spend money on coaching

*Why?*

Because the economy is bad, because everyone's struggling to make ends meet, because coaching is a luxury for most people...

Once you start doing this for each reason, excuse or story you've come up with, you'll begin to notice a pattern.

It was while I was doing this excavation work that I truly came face to face with my belief in lack (see Introduction, page 5). When I took a good and honest look at the excuses I'd given myself, I realised each one was based on things I felt I didn't have: lack of knowledge, lack of prospective clients, lack of opportunities in a tough economy, lack of resources, lack of time, etc. When I dug even deeper to find out whether this belief in lack affected other areas of my life, I shocked myself. I realised that even when I was earning good money and had disposable income plus savings in the bank, I still never felt I had enough. So life was never OK because I was often worried about needing to earn more money, resented having to spend money or obsessed over every penny.

Now that you've got an idea of how to uncover the limiting beliefs behind the reasons why you can't have what you want, note down what comes to mind. What are the excuses, reasons or stories you tell yourself as to why you can't have what you want? What pattern emerges from these stories? And what might be the limiting belief at their core?

## Where do limiting beliefs come from?

Having identified the pattern in your excuses and the limiting belief behind them, ask yourself: where did this limiting belief come from?

Remember, we didn't come into the world with a host of beliefs in tow. We form them according to the meanings we give to our experiences, and often as children we take on the beliefs of the significant adults around us. So it makes total sense to question where a belief, particularly a limiting one, came from. For example, I realised my belief in lack came from my dad because I remember how obsessed he was with not having enough money despite the fact we always had plenty. Although he earned a good salary throughout his working life, he was always reluctant to spend money. I remember him spending ages deliberating over buying something and how my mum would despair if she ever wanted to buy new things for the home, never mind paying for home improvements.

In the end she went to back to work so that she could earn the money to spend on whatever she wanted. Even then, she'd sometimes get the third degree from dad. In our household, the glass was always half empty, so that sense of lack, that feeling of there never being enough became part of my very existence. Without questioning it (because I hadn't experienced anything different), I took on a belief in lack.

When I finally understood where this limiting belief came from, and how it had formed, it was liberating to realise I could play around with it and question it. Why? Because by identifying the origin of my limiting belief, I could ask myself: do I *really* believe this here and now? Is this belief true to who I am now? And most importantly: do I want to hold on to this belief?

Asking myself these questions opened up new channels for me. After my personal wake-up call, I absolutely wanted to live life to my full potential. No way was that going to be possible if I continued believing in lack. And I knew deep down that if I held onto this belief, I'd only have myself to blame for holding *me* back. The most important thing I learned was that I had a choice. Beliefs don't just happen and own you – *you* choose the extent to which a belief rules your life.

### Questioning your limiting beliefs

Once you've identified the limiting belief that's holding you back, ask yourself:

- Is this belief really true for me now?

- Am I absolutely convinced it's true for me now?

- What's it like when I hold this belief? (Really explore how you see, hear and feel the world *with* this belief.)

- Would I teach this belief to young children?

- What would it be like if I no longer held this belief? (Explore how you might see, hear and feel the world *without* this belief.)

- Knowing there are now different possibilities, do I still want to hold on to this belief?

Recap – how to find the limiting beliefs that are stopping you:

1. Question your reasons, stories and excuses. For each one, ask why?
2. Study your reasons why. Look for patterns.
3. Identify the pattern and the limiting belief behind it.
4. Ask yourself where this limiting belief may have come from.
5. Run through the questions above to assess whether this limiting belief is still true for you now and whether it's appropriate to hang on to it.

## CHAPTER 5

# POSITIVE INTENT

OF course, it's tempting to try to get rid of something we no longer want, so as soon as we've identified a limiting belief, the natural reaction is to disown it, banish it, lock it away and hide the key. As tempting as this might be, it's actually counter-productive, because banishing something to the shadows will only make it come back in ways that can often take us by surprise:

> *It is a frightening thought that man also has a shadow side to him, consisting not just of little weaknesses – and foibles, but of a positively demonic dynamism. The individual seldom knows anything of this....But let these harmless creatures form a mass, and there emerges a raging monster...*
>
> *On the Psychology of the Unconscious (1912), Carl Jung*

For this precise reason, it's important to recognise that every limiting belief actually carries a *positive intention* for us. By discovering and acknowledging what that positive intention is, and making sure we honour that intent in our lives, we're then better able to start letting go of, or at least revising, the limiting belief.

Identifying limiting beliefs and the positive intention behind them can be challenging, so it's often best to work with an experienced therapist or coach who can guide you and provide an objective view. But if you're working on your own for the moment, try doing more excavation work (see Chapter 4, p57).

Take some time out to continue exploring your limiting belief. By the end of the previous chapter, you'll already have explored in some depth what it's like to hold this belief. Now think about its positive intent for you. Could it be looking out for you in some way? If so, in what way might it be protecting or looking after you? What is it trying to protect you from?

## Transforming a limiting belief

When I tried to discover the positive intent

behind my limiting belief in lack, I realised it was all about keeping me safe. Believing in lack meant I was generally limiting and restricting myself. I was stopping myself from letting go and taking risks. Not taking risks meant I could stay safe.

Once I had acknowledged that and accepted I wanted to start letting go of my belief in lack, I focused on how I could do that and still feel safe. For me, this meant concentrating on three key things:

- Connecting with and being fully present in the now

- Relating differently and more lightly to my thoughts and feelings

- Being more aware of my self-talk.

It's worth keeping all of the above elements in mind when you're aiming to transform a limiting belief and retain its positive intent, because limiting beliefs don't tend to give up that easily. After all, they've been ingrained for a long time and we all know that old habits die hard. That's why it's important to acknowledge the positive intent behind the limiting belief, so that we recognise part of its raison d'être and, in so doing, ease the grip it's had on our thoughts, feelings and self-talk.

### *Connecting with and being fully present now*

To what extent are you totally present in the now? Are you truly present in this moment physically, emotionally and mentally, or are you 'here but not quite'? We all know that feeling when we may be physically present but our thoughts and/or emotions are elsewhere. You may be sitting in a meeting with colleagues, but your thoughts are focused on the long to-do list that's waiting for you on your desk. You may be listening to a friend talking about their problems, but underneath you're still pissed off and obsessing about the negative comment your partner made earlier that morning.

We all do it, but often our ability to be 'here but not quite' is more of a disadvantage than a useful skill. It's the difference between living life to the full and merely existing. Why? Take yourself back to a moment when you felt truly alive. What was that like? What did it feel like?

Often when I ask clients to recall these moments, I get comments such as: 'I was totally there taking in everything around me', 'I was in the zone', 'It felt amazing like all my sensations were heightened', 'It felt great – I felt confident and at one with myself'.

When we allow ourselves to be present, we invite a different essence and quality of attention into the moment. Being present brings those feelings we've all experienced at one time or another of being totally engrossed in the moment, sensing and feeling everything and everyone around us. It can feel exhilarating and exciting or beautifully calming, joyful and peaceful.

The mere act of taking a deep breath and sensing the effect this has on your body is an easy step to being more present in the now. Extend that further and you'll be amazed.

Practising 'presence' was really important for me when I was experimenting with letting go of my belief in lack, yet still feeling safe. Whenever I found myself worrying about not feeling safe because of a perceived risk I'd taken or was about to take, I'd force myself back into the present moment. I'd take a deep breath, bring my energy and thoughts back to myself instead of having them racing away into a presumed (not actual) future and I'd focus on the present moment. Then I'd literally ask myself: am I safe here and now? And all the time the answer would be: Right here, right now, yes, I am safe. I'm paying my bills and getting by OK, so yes, I'm safe and it's OK.

Knowing I'm safe now – and having evidence of other times in the past when I was indeed safe – would help dissipate any fears of not being safe in the future. It would also help bring my energy back into the present (which I have some control over) and away from the future (which I can't control because I can't predict what will happen).

When you're experimenting with letting go of a limiting belief and its positive intent feels at risk in some way, eg feeling unsafe, vulnerable or out of control, try being more present in the now. Take a deep breath in and a full breath out. Do this at least twice more. As you inhale, imagine yourself bringing your energy back in to yourself. Call back all those thoughts and feelings that may be racing out into the future or the past. And as you exhale, centre yourself wherever you are and feel your energy rooting itself into the present moment. Once you feel well rooted in the present, ask yourself: how safe, strong, in control, etc am I right here and now in this very moment? Gather evidence that this is the case right here and now. If you need to, write the evidence down for reinforcement.

### Relating differently and more lightly with your thoughts and feelings

Until I practised meditation and mindfulness, I was often drowning in my own thoughts. I'd have a constant internal dialogue churning away, generating thought after thought about completely inane things or, if I was having a particularly bad day, about all the other things that could go wrong before the day was up: 'I bet this bloody bus will get caught in traffic, so I'll be even more late. What if I miss the meeting, what will happen then? Why's that guy looking at me funny? I bet you he's talking about me to his friend. She didn't acknowledge me in the lift – she must be pissed off about something.'

Often, too, I'd let myself get carried away by my feelings, particularly if they were negative ones, such as anger, resentment or disappointment. I'd get totally consumed by them and it would take ages (sometimes years) to let go of them completely.

When I eventually realised how stressed and miserable I was by allowing my thoughts and feelings to take over my life completely, I set out to change things. The practice in meditation of noting and observing thoughts without judgement was a helpful start, as was the knowledge and acceptance that we are all more than our thoughts and feelings.

What exactly does that mean? Take a moment to revisit your list of values (see p25). These values are an essential part of who you are. They alone amount to much more than any thought you might have, such as – what you're going to do when you finish reading this, or feelings of anger or frustration. Remember, our values are an essential, enduring part of us; thoughts and feelings come and go.

Once we start to accept that our thoughts and feelings are just that and no more, they needn't mean much unless we want them to. By accepting that we are *more* than them, we begin to experience them more lightly. This is very important when we start letting go of, or updating, a limiting belief.

In my case, whenever I feel unsafe, I say this to myself: 'Can you sense that this feeling of not being safe is just a thought or feeling and that you are more than that? Knowing this, can you let go of the feeling of not being safe?'

Again, this process can be smoother and easier with the support of a coach or therapist, but if you're initially working on your own, try gaining an 'observer's' perspective on your thoughts and feelings, and practise getting a sense that you are much more than them.

## Being aware of your self-talk

As you will have noticed above, our self-talk or internal dialogue can be dominated by our thoughts and feelings, predominantly the negative ones. At the same time, self-talk can also be influenced by our limiting beliefs.

Self-talk is negative and self-critical 99% of the time and, until we start to explore it properly, we assume there's very little we can do about the constant grief we give ourselves.

Because that inner voice is often critical, nagging and downright rude, it's tempting to try to squash it, banish it and silence it as much as possible. But isn't it funny how, the moment you do that, the voice seems to get louder and more persistent? The trick is to start noting and observing this inner voice in a way similar to how we did so above.

Instead of trying to block or ignore your self-talk, try acknowledging it for a change. Get curious about it. When does it pipe up? What does it tend to say? What's the tone and quality of the voice? Where do you hear the voice – to your left, to your right, from the centre? Whose voice is it? A lot of people say it's their own voice but others say it's someone else's like mum's, dad's or a teacher's, for example.

Once you start to explore your self-talk, you'll be surprised at how its quality begins to change. It's almost as if, at the moment we really start to listen, it calms down a little and begins to interact with us more – it talks *to* us instead of *at* us. Most of my clients experience a sense of relief when they begin to acknowledge and have a dialogue with their inner voice. Often, they realise that the inner voice they used to experience as critical, nagging and rude actually has a positive intent, like our limiting beliefs (see p64). In many cases that positive intent is to look after us. With that in mind, I often encourage clients to think of their inner voice more as a 'critical friend'. In other words, the criticism may not go away completely, but it's there because your inner voice is in fact a friend whose intent is to look after you and keep you safe.

When you become more aware of this, you can start to have a better relationship with your inner voice. You can play with and respond to it: 'Thank you, yes, I hear you, and I know you've got my best interests at heart. At the same time, I know I did the right thing/it wasn't such a mistake/I'm not as stupid as you say I am.'

By acknowledging our inner voice and its positive intent, and by engaging in dialogue with it, we begin to take back control. When I was dealing with my limiting beliefs, it was really useful for me to discover the origin, qualities and intent of my self-talk, because instead of feeling under constant attack or criticism, I was gradually able to respond and stand up for myself.

## Recap

When you're aiming to transform a limiting belief and its positive intent may feel under threat:

- Connect with and be fully present now. Often, when you centre yourself in the present moment, the perceived threat lessens

- Remember, your thoughts and feelings are just temporary and that you are more than them

- Explore your self-talk – begin to have a dialogue and engage with your 'critical friend'.

## CHAPTER 6

# CREATING OR UPDATING BELIEFS

PERSONALLY, I love the definition of beliefs as 'our current best thinking', because it leaves room for us to modify that thinking if we choose to. If a certain limiting belief has constantly been tripping you up, working against you or quite simply ruining your chances of living a fulfilling life, wouldn't you want to modify or update it, once you've understood and acknowledged the positive intent behind it?

This, by far, was the one big revelation that blew my mind, because it opened up so many possibilities I'd convinced myself I didn't have. My beliefs had become such a part of myself and my existence that I never even questioned whether they could be updated.

So how do we go about either updating our limiting beliefs or creating new, more empowering ones?

First of all, look back at a limiting belief you identified in Chapter 4 (see p59). Be aware, too, of the positive intent behind the belief. Knowing what you know now, what would be a more empowering belief to have? Write down the first thing that comes to mind. As you look at what you've written down, begin to connect with your new belief: what will you see, hear and feel around you as you go about the world with this new belief? What will your friends and family see, hear and feel when you're around them?

Try the new belief out for size. This may take some time and feel unusual at first, but that's OK, because you're getting used to a new way of thinking and being. At this point, it may be useful to hone in on three important centres within you: your head, your heart and your gut.

## Aligning your centres

Have you ever been faced with a decision and found that your head is keen to go for it but your heart's not so sure or your gut doesn't quite feel right about it? This used to happen to me a lot whenever I had to make a decision about a job. My head would be raring to go for it, thinking about the new challenge ahead, and of course the bigger pay packet, but my gut would be sending out 'not really sure about this' signals. I'd be aware of the signals and sometimes I'd even try to understand them, but my head always won out. In the end, when I got frustrated and fed up with the job, I'd ask myself: 'Why the hell didn't you listen to your gut in the first place? You'd obviously picked up that something was not quite right, but too late now!'

Too late indeed. Unfortunately, this pattern repeated itself several times in my career until I finally learnt to listen to my gut and my heart, as well as my head. By listening to and acknowledging all three, I was learning to be more aligned and therefore more congruent.

When we find ourselves floundering or downright stuck, it's often because there's a misalignment or even conflict between our three centres: My head says I should stay in this relationship but my heart says not. My head says I should stay in this country where all my friends and family are but my heart is drawn elsewhere. My head says I should go with the invasive treatment but my gut feels there may be another way.

Whenever we need to make a big decision or change in our lives, it's often a good idea to check in with head, heart and gut. To do this, try working your way through the following checklist:

Think of a goal you'd like to achieve and make a note of it here:

For each statement below, check in with head, heart and gut, and rate how strongly each centre feels in relation to the statement. 1 is lowest and 5 is strongest.

*My goal is important to me and I want to reach it.*

**Head**

**Heart**

**Gut**

*It's possible to reach my goal.*

**Head**

**Heart**

**Gut**

*I'm capable of reaching my goal.*

**Head**

**Heart**

**Gut**

*I deserve to reach my goal.*

**Head**

**Heart**

**Gut**


Now look at your scores. If you've scored 5 for every statement, congratulations, you're fully aligned and congruent. That's the ideal scenario, but reality is often far from ideal. It won't be surprising to find that you've scored one centre high and the others low.

Where this is the case, look again at the statement. Hone in on the centre or centres that have scored low and ask yourself: what else would I need to know, add to my goal or believe in to be more congruent or confident? Take note of your answer and explore how you can make this possible. As with some exercises in previous chapters, it's often easier to work with a coach or therapist.

When you're trying your new belief out for size, it's useful to take it through the process set out above. Whatever your new more empowering belief is, check it out with head, heart and gut. Then, you also need to find out what your 'critical friend' has to say about this new belief. Check for any doubts or objections. Are they valid? If so, are there any tweaks or changes you need to make?

As you go about the world with your new belief, check and make sure that the original positive intent is still being honoured and kept. For example, if the positive intent was to keep you safe, is your new empowering belief still allowing you to feel that way?

It's also worth bearing in mind that if you want a new empowering belief to really 'stick', it needs to meet the following conditions:

- The belief is a positive statement. For example, I have the inner strength to deal with difficult situations *vs* I don't have to be afraid of difficult situations.

- The belief gives you behavioural choices. For example, I'm OK when I'm up high (good because this is generalised and can apply to all situations when you're up high) *vs* I'm OK when I'm on a plane (not so good as this could imply: but I may not be relaxed when I'm standing near the edge of a tall building).

- It's a belief, not a behaviour. For example, I'm loveable as I am *vs* I can get love from others.

- It's a simple statement that even kids would understand.

- There's no predictable downside to holding this new belief. For example, difficult situations don't frighten me *vs* I have the inner strength to deal with difficult situations – this is better as it implies you have more control and choice over how you respond to a situation.

- It allows possibility (see example above).


Once it meets all of the above conditions, be sure to write it down once, twice, several times, in fact, so that it can really begin to sink in.

As I mentioned at the beginning of this book, one of the limiting beliefs I had and wanted to update was: I'm not good enough. Ironically, I discovered the positive intent behind that belief was for me to avoid disappointment. In other words, if ever anyone rejected me (and I became very adept at creating situations for this to happen consistently), I could put it down to the fact I was never good enough in the first place. Of course, this led to a very limited and sometimes painful experience of life.

After a number of coaching sessions, I eventually embraced the more empowering belief of: I am good enough. For me, the word 'enough' is important, because not only does it counteract the limiting belief I had around lack (there is never enough), but it also addresses the positive intent to avoid disappointment – if I am 'enough', how can I ever be disappointed?

## Recap

To create or update a belief:

- Be aware of the positive intent behind the limiting belief you want to update

- Work on crafting a more empowering belief

- Connect with the new empowering belief – what will you feel, hear and see around you with this new belief?

- Check in with head, heart and gut – what's their response to the new belief?

- Check in with your 'critical friend'

- Make adjustments as necessary

- Make sure the original positive intent is still being honoured.

Chapter 7

# LEARNING TO BE AT PEACE
# WITH YOURSELF

WE want to let go of limiting beliefs and develop and embrace more empowering ones so that we can begin to experience life and the many opportunities it presents to us more fully. The one thing I've learnt both by working on myself and with clients is that working on transforming limiting beliefs is all the more successful once we truly learn to be at peace with ourselves.

But what exactly does being at peace with oneself mean? During my years as a generally functioning yet dysfunctional adult, I came across tons of advice about the benefits of practising inner peace. From spiritual healing groups, to Tai Chi classes, to leaders in the spiritual and personal development fields, I often came across quotes like these:

*'We can never obtain peace in the outer world until we make peace with ourselves.'*

The Dalai Lama

*'Peace begins with me. The more peaceful I am inside, the more peace I have to share with others.'*

Louise Hay

*'When you're at peace with yourself and you love yourself, it's virtually impossible for you to do things to yourself that are destructive.'*

Wayne Dyer

Like many other people, I'd take the words in and process them intellectually. Sometimes, I may have even meditated to create some temporary sense of inner peace, but I never really *grasped* what inner peace actually involved. I think this has a lot to do with the fact that the term 'inner peace' has become so generalised in our culture. Mention the term and almost immediately many people will think about Buddha, the Dalai Lama, doing yoga or a recent article they saw on mindfulness. Many of us have formed a general impression of what 'inner peace' is, but when asked how you go about achieving it, or even how you know when you've got it, very few of us can say for sure.

This chapter looks at the components that make up the concept of 'inner peace' and the practical steps to understanding and living it.

## Letting go of self-criticism

Think back to Chapter 5 and the section on being aware of your self-talk. If you're constantly criticising, nagging or cursing yourself, how at peace are you really? Many of us, without being consciously aware of it, are walking around under constant internal attack from ourselves. If we're already putting ourselves under such pressure from the inside, how are we likely to react if someone or something challenges us on the outside? You've been in that sort of situation before, haven't you? All you're aware of inside is that really annoying voice that keeps criticising everything you do and say, and then, all of a sudden, your partner, boss or a complete stranger says something you don't like – and you explode.

I finally decided to do something about my own self-criticism when I realised how constantly at odds I seemed to be with the outside world. I was having regular arguments with my partner, run-ins with neighbours and tetchy exchanges with colleagues and clients. Feeling at a loss as to how to deal with it all, and realising that deep down all these arguments and run-ins were ultimately making me feel criticised and judged, I asked myself: What would happen if *you* stopped criticising yourself? What would happen if you stopped giving yourself a hard time about your weight? About having that piece of cake instead of a healthier snack? Resting instead of going for a run or working out? Taking time off instead of working on this book? And all those other things you're so good at giving yourself a hard time about?

As well as acknowledging that inner voice and engaging in dialogue with it, I took things a step further and made an active effort to stop criticising myself. The moment I started doing that, the moment I began to let myself off the hook, things began to change. Because I was cutting down on giving myself such a hard time, I found I became more relaxed towards other people as well. The moment I stopped criticising myself and expecting so much from myself (and letting myself down), I was more able to accept people as they are, instead of expecting them to act in a certain way – and then feeling let down or disappointed when they didn't.

## Start letting yourself off the hook now

How do you even begin to let go of self-criticism? A good place to start is by understanding that the outside world is often a reflection of our inner world. That's what's meant by the saying: As above, so below, *as within, so without…* [my italics]

If the outside world is indeed a mirror, imagine that it's reflecting back the results of your thoughts and ideas. What does what you're seeing say about you? How are your current thoughts being represented by external reality? Do you like what you see and is it what you really want? These are the questions I asked myself when I felt at odds with everything and everyone around me.

Try asking yourself these questions and answering as honestly as you can. Write your answers down. You may be surprised at what comes up, but you'll end up with clues about what might need your attention.

Next, monitor your thoughts and self-talk. In Chapter 5 we learnt the importance of acknowledging our inner voice, identifying its positive intent and engaging in dialogue with it. The next step is to monitor when that inner voice is about to go into critical or nagging mode and interrupting it. You can start by acknowledging it: 'Yes, thank you, I hear what you're saying and I'm OK as I am, thanks.' Gradually try softening the tone and message it's giving you. After all, most of the time you wouldn't dream of talking to your children or a young baby that way, so why do it to yourself in the first place?

Instead of saying to myself, 'What the hell do you think you're doing having a rest instead of going for a run – you'll end up getting fatter than you already are!', I'd start answering with: 'Yep, that's right, I'm sure a day off running won't do me any harm.' Then, next time, I'd remind myself not to give myself such a hard time, so my answer would become a question instead: 'Are you happy to have a rest day today?' Eventually, I'd let myself off the hook completely.

You'll be amazed at the effect changing the way you think about and talk to yourself can have. Once you start letting yourself off the hook, your whole physiology begins to change – areas of tension loosen up, you begin to breathe more deeply and you no longer feel pulled in different directions. Because you're no longer focusing on what's wrong with you or what's wrong with other people, you're no longer attracting the situations that reflect that. Remember – *as within, so without.* Quite simply, you're in a much better place to simply be at peace.

## Accepting where you are in the present moment

When you begin to be at peace with yourself, you'll begin to understand what it's truly like to be in the present moment. Why? Because once you start freeing your mind from most of the nagging thoughts, self-criticism and expectations (both of yourself and others) that used to fill it, there's more space to appreciate the here and now.

When you're no longer criticising yourself and other people, you start to appreciate the stuff that's actually good in your life. Yes, believe it or not, there is good stuff around, if you allow yourself to look for it and see it.

## The true power of feeling and being grateful

Like the concept of inner peace, 'practising gratitude' can seem elusive. Again, lots of leaders and teachers in the spiritual and personal development field talk about how important it is to practise gratitude, but because the concept doesn't truly connect or resonate with many people, it remains another of those generalised thoughts.

There is, however, a growing bank of scientific research around the science of the heart, particularly from the Institute of HeartMath (www.heartmath.org). This research shows that the heart is actually much more than a simple pump:

*The heart is, in fact, a highly complex, self-organised information processing center with its own functional "brain" that communicates with and influences the cranial brain via the nervous system and other pathways. These influences profoundly affect brain function and most of the body's organs, and ultimately determine the quality of life....*

*It became clear that negative emotions lead to increased disorder in the heart's rhythms and in the autonomic nervous system, thereby adversely affecting the rest of the body. In contrast, positive emotions create increased harmony and coherence in heart rhythms and improve balance in the nervous system.*

*Science of the Heart: Exploring the Role of the Heart in Human Performance*

Institute of HeartMath

This last paragraph alone begins to explain a) the holistic effect letting go of self-criticism can have and b) why practising gratitude can indeed be good for us.

Think about it: isn't it true that a lot of the time we instinctively focus on what we don't have? 'I wish I had a partner, I wish I had more money, I wish I had a better job…'

Yet, if internally our minds are full of thoughts about what we don't want, surely we'll only keep seeing more of the same in the outside world? *As within, so without…*

What might happen if we actively started focusing on what we're thankful for?

Try it. At the very least, focusing on what you do have and are grateful for will have a more positive effect on your heart and whole body. At the very most, it might begin to bring more of the experiences, people and things you do want into your life.

## Practical ways to practise gratitude

There are a number of ways to practise gratitude, including: keeping a gratitude list and the circle of gratitude.

### *Keeping a gratitude list*

One of the simplest ways to practise gratitude is by jotting down a gratitude list as regularly as you can. Find yourself a notebook or simply use the list or notes function on your smartphone, whatever's easiest. Dedicate a time of day to writing down or typing at least 10 things you're grateful for. Some people like to add to their list throughout the day, others find it easier to do it at the end of the day. Your list can be as simple or as general as you like, as long as it records what you're grateful for, for example:

I'm grateful for:

- A good night's sleep
- My early morning run in the sun
- The lovely breakfast my wife cooked for me
- The person who smiled at me on the train this morning
- Having a really productive meeting
- Having a good chat with a friend over lunch
- Getting a seat on the train home, even though it was busy
- A nutritious, home-cooked dinner
- Having time to relax and read
- My new, soft and comfortable pillow.

When I first started making my gratitude lists, it felt a bit odd. We're all so wired to hone in on what's wrong in our lives that focusing on what's good (even the little things) may seem childish, flaky or even 'New Agey'. I get that because that's exactly how I felt and yet, at the same time, I thought why not give it a go? Why not experiment and see if focusing on the good things (instead of all the bad things) will indeed bring more good things into your life? It could be worth a try, couldn't it?

Once you really get into your gratitude lists and see them making incremental differences in your life, you might want to try the circle of gratitude to amplify further the power of the heart in gratitude.

### Circle of gratitude

Heartfelt thanks go to Tim Hallbom of NLP California for introducing me to this process.

Find a space where you won't be interrupted. You'll need enough physical space to be able to stand in one area and then in another directly in front of that area. Once you've found a suitable space, stand tall and do whatever feels natural to feel centred and completely present in that space. You may want to take a few deep breaths. As you breathe in, feel yourself taking energy into every part of your body. As you breathe out, feel your feet strongly connected to the ground.

When you feel fully present and centred in your space, imagine a circle of gratitude on the ground right in front of you. With your eyes closed or open (whichever feels most comfortable), observe that circle of gratitude. How big is it? What texture is it? What colour is it? What level of brightness and/or depth does it have?

Once you get a real feel for that circle of gratitude, think about something or someone you're truly and deeply grateful for right now. See that something or someone you're truly grateful for in your circle of gratitude right now. See what you see, feel what you feel, hear what you hear.

Now step into your circle of gratitude and be totally present in it. As you breathe in, see, feel and hear that sense of gratitude. As you breathe out, feel your heart fill your circle with even more gratitude.

Breathe in and feel that sense of gratitude; breathe out and, this time, fill the room you're in with gratitude.

Breathe in and feel that sense of gratitude; breathe out and fill the building you're in with gratitude.

Repeat this to amplify and expand your sense of gratitude to your neighbourhood, your city, your region, your country, the continent, the world, even the universe.

When you're aware of amplifying your gratitude to the universe, gather up all the other gratitude that's out there and bring it back to yourself in your own circle of gratitude.

Practising gratitude can be powerful and it can also bring us further along the journey of being at peace with ourselves. Practising gratitude can be as simple and as powerful as acknowledging: I'm grateful to be alive. Yet how often do we ever stop even to acknowledge that pure and simple fact?

Once you practise gratitude enough in your day-to-day life, you may even want to start asking yourself the question: What would happen if I believed I have everything I want and need in this present moment? You know the answer: I'd be more at peace with myself and everything and everyone around me.

## Don't give your power away

As well as the concept of inner peace, another idea I remember grasping intellectually but not quite in practice was: don't give your (personal) power away. Again, it's a concept that a lot of leaders in the personal and spiritual development field write and talk about. In essence, our ability to stay centred and hold our power is another key to inner peace but what does it mean to give your power away and how does giving it away actually affect us?

Here's a personal story that gave me a new understanding of how we inadvertently give our power away.

A few years ago, we had a fall-out with our neighbours after we'd done some building work they didn't like. It was quite a big fall-out, which was a shame because before the building work, we'd got on well and saw each other socially from time to time. After the fall-out, things got extremely frosty. They stopped acknowledging us in the street and if we did bump into each other and said hello, we'd get a laboured hello back, if we were lucky.

I personally found this difficult a) because I

fundamentally believed we hadn't done anything wrong and b) because I couldn't reconcile how warm and friendly they'd been with us beforehand with how they were still behaving two years on: angry and resentful. As a result, to avoid coming across their continued anger and resentment, I'd consciously avoid them whenever I knew our paths might cross.

This meant that one Saturday each month, when I had to go into town early, I'd go through the following charade: I knew they both worked on Saturdays, usually got the same train as me and got off at the same destination. So, whenever I arrived at the station, I'd make a point of standing to one side of the platform to let them walk past without noticing me. I'd worked out that they always got on towards the front of the train to avoid a long walk to the ticket gates at the other end, so I'd board the train in the middle.

This is a classic example of giving one's power away, although I didn't see it like that back then. To me, I was taking steps to avoid an awkward and unpleasant situation, because I knew they'd be frosty with me as usual. Also, had it been just one of them, I would have been able to cope, but both of them exuding frostiness and resentment was too much. This little charade continued for months.

Then, one Saturday, I left the house a little later than usual. As I was walking to the station, I heard voices not far behind me and realised it was them. When I crossed the road at my usual spot, I caught a glimpse of them walking past to cross further down the road, so I knew they'd seen me. I ended up on the station platform before them. As usual, I stood to one side, waiting for them to walk past but they didn't. For a moment, I wondered if they weren't taking the usual train but, having observed them for months, it was clear they were creatures of habit, so it would be unusual for them to change their normal pattern.

Something told me to walk further up the platform in full view, which I did, and when I turned around, I caught a glimpse of them hanging back. When the train arrived, they boarded towards the back.

As I sat on the train I had a profound 'a-ha' moment. They'd clearly seen me walking towards the station and, once there, they'd seen me further up the platform and deliberately chose to hang back. It was at that point that I totally understood and felt the concept of giving one's power away. On this occasion, two grown men had actually modified their normal behaviour (walking to the front of the platform and getting on at the front of the train to have a shorter walk to the ticket gate on arrival), and in doing so had given their power away to me, without me even being conscious of it.

The irony was, of course, that all along I'd been giving my power away by modifying my behaviour because I was fearful of coming across both of them, yet here they were, to my mind enjoying 'safety in numbers' but, in fact, avoiding little old me. It was at that precise moment that a) I completely understood the consequences of giving one's power away and b) I resolved consciously to avoid doing so as much as possible, because ultimately the only person who really suffers is <u>me</u>.

Think about it – how often do you give your power away? How often have you stayed angry at someone? Kept blaming someone or something for what's happened to you? Kept complaining about the way someone's treated you? How often have you modified your own behaviour because of the grudges and bad feelings you're hanging on to?

Has hanging on to the anger, the blame and the complaints in any way affected or changed the people or situations you've been directing those feelings towards? Who *is* actually affected by those feelings? Who carries them around in their head 24/7? You do. Now tell me: is it really worth it?

## *Where are you giving your power away?*

We don't just give our power away (often obliviously) to other people. Sometimes, situations or things we do can drain us of energy and drive. Try the following exercise to better identify what's draining you and therefore giving your power away.

Take a moment to reflect on situations and/or people that might cause you to give your power away. Think about all your relationships, ways of being, beliefs, attitudes, behaviours, habits and even material things. List what comes up for you now:

For this next stage, focus on two typical days and make a note of your activities from the moment you get up to the moment you go to bed. Focusing on half-hour increments, identify what's draining you and what's nourishing you.

Once you've completed this stage, you'll be able to work out which activities you may want to start letting go of because they're draining you and no longer serve you. At the same time, you'll have a pretty good idea of the activities that do serve and nurture you. Work out how you can fit more of these into your daily routine. Make a list of what nurtures you and add to it. Keep the list safe and refer back to it often. Think of your 'nurturing' list as your compass – whenever you start to feel a little bit out of kilter, be sure to do one or two things on your list.

By letting yourself off the hook more, learning to be in the present moment, practising gratitude and giving less of your power away, you begin to take the necessary steps to being more at peace with yourself.

# CHAPTER 8

# CONCLUSION

*Argue your limitations and sure enough they're yours*

Richard Bach

IT seems appropriate at this point to re-ask the question: so what's stopping you from starting again and getting what you want? By now I hope you're beginning to realise a lot of the limitations we believe are 'out there' actually live inside us and are therefore self-imposed.

What's more, you now have the steps and resources to start moving beyond them:

a) Be clear on who and what you're about (what's important to you?)

b) Identify what it is you want and why (make sure it's compelling enough)

c) Be honest about what's stopping you from getting what you want

d) Explore and identify what limiting beliefs are stopping you from getting what you want

e) Work out what the positive intent is behind the limiting belief

f) Craft an updated, more empowering belief, making sure it keeps the positive intent of the previous limiting belief

g) Practise being at peace with yourself, being present and feeling gratitude daily.

By following these steps you'll begin to feel that life begins to flow more as you become much more present, connected and engaged with everyone and everything around you.

What's more, you'll feel more confident about discovering the true you and starting over again. And remember, you're a work in progress, so keep revisiting the tools in this book, sign up to my website (www.jackiemendoza.com) to receive free resources or to hear about new talks and seminars, and, above all, enjoy!

*Human beings are works in progress that mistakenly think they're finished*

Dan Gilbert

## Resources

If you'd like to take what you've learnt in this book further, you can contact the author direct via www.jackiemendoza.com or sign up for free resources at the same web address.

If you're interested in NLP and Applied Neuroscience, visit www.itsnlp.com for training courses and more.

# About the Author

JACKIE MENDOZA is a change coach and seminar leader working with people who want to rebuild their lives when a relationship changes or ends (marriage/partnership, children growing up, or a change in career or profession). Jackie is a certified NLP Master Practitioner as well as a certified Practitioner in Applied Neuroscience. She has also trained as a counsellor (Transpersonal perspective) and spiritual healer and uses a variety of these influences in her work.